Seducer's Guide to "Hypnopoetics...Modern Love Poems and Hypnotic Inductions"

Second Edition

by Phil Billitz

Version 3.2
Copyright 2014 – all rights reserved
4 Quarters Technology, LLC

PLEASE NOTE: This "Seducer's Guide" is a COMPANION guide to
"Hypnopoetics...Modern Love Poems and Hypnotic Inductions"
It won't be very helpful to you without the "Hypnopoetics" book.

Also by the Author:

Hypnopoetics Books:
- Right Now - a Hypno Poem (Kindle) A single Hypno Poem with complete explanation
- Certainly - a Hypno Poem (Kindle) A single Hypno Poem with complete explanation
- Hypnopoetics: Poèmes Hypnotiques de Séduction Hypnotique (French Edition) (Kindle & Paperback)

Photo Books:
- DSLR Photography - Antelope Canyon (Kindle and Paperback) Photo Book and Travel Guide
- Antique Car Hood Ornaments **(Kindle)** Photo Book

Join the Hypnopoetics Pre-Release Book Group to participate in readings and discussions, to receive free and discounted books of Hypnotic Seduction Poetry... And learn how you can be named in the Acknowledgements for the New Book!

Click to Join the "Hypnopoetics..." Pre-Release Book Group

Table of Contents

New for the Second Edition –
- replaced tables with text explanations of the poems. The tables did not display well across all devices.
- identified the Embedded commands used in all the poems
- listed the poems in the order that they appear in "Hypnopoetics…"
- provided a FAQ or frequently asked questions section
- provided links to videos with examples of how to use the poems
- provided a section on "How to Write Your Own Hypno Poems"

PLEASE NOTE: This "Seducer's Guide" is a COMPANION guide to "Hypnopoetics…Modern Love Poems and Hypnotic Inductions". IT IS NOT A STAND-ALONE WORK IN AND OF ITSELF.

The "Seducer's Guide to Hypnopoetics" is the **User's Guide** and **Instruction Manual** for "Hypnopoetics… Modern Love Poems and Hypnotic Inductions."

It tells you how and when to use the Hypno Poems in "Hypnopoetics…" and also tells you how to create your own. It also discusses in detail the structure of the Hypno Poems and how to write your own Hypnotic Seduction Poetry.

Buy this after you get your hands on some of my hypno poems and are interested in understanding HOW they work. To be honest, it won't be very helpful to you without the "Hypnopoetics…" book.

One early reviewer on Amazon was very critical of the "Seducer's Guide", apparently he didn't get the memo.

As many, many happy seducers have found, Hypno poems are easy to read and use. This **Seducer's Guide** will assist you in getting the maximum benefit from the powerful Hypnotic Seduction Poems in "Hypnopoetics… Modern Love Poems and Hypnotic Inductions"

thanks,
Phil
P.S. In this Guide, and in the Hypno Poems, I use the feminine gender to refer to the person who is listening to the poem. If your spouse/lover/heart's desire is not female, feel free to read the poems with whatever gender is more appropriate to your situation.

Do You Have to Read Them Out Loud?

There are a number of ways to deliver the Hypno Poems, and not all of these ways are equally effective.

Here are some delivery options, from most effective to least effective:
1. read or recite the poem in person while using nlp anchoring techniques
2. read or recite the poem over the phone
3. write or print out the poem and give it to her
4. send the poem in an email or post on her facebook wall
5. send pieces of the poem to her as txt messages

To be most effective, you should ALWAYS READ THE POEMS ALOUD to her. The key to understanding why is that when you read the poem aloud to her, you are anchoring the Hypno Poems emotions, images and state of mind to YOU and YOUR VOICE.

Here is how I would do it:
1. Read (or better yet, recite) one and if you see her responding well, you know you are on to something
2. Pay attention to the response that you are getting. I doubt that it will be effective to read someone a series of these if they are distracted or just not getting into it.
3. Ask her how the poem made her feel – listen carefully and utilize the information in further conversation

On paper or posted to a web page, a Hypno Poem may come across as a cool poem, but it just won't be as hypnotic and associative. The poem might impress her, but you may lose that powerful connection and association to YOU that a verbal, hypnotic delivery will accomplish.

What if she is thinking of someone else when she reads it, or what if the internal feelings are generated, but not anchored to your voice? Believe me, creating a lot of free-floating erotic emotions in someone without anchoring them to YOU is not optimal.

Will These Work on My Spouse/Lover/Heart's Desire?

Studies at Stanford University have estimated that only that 20% to 25% of the population can't be hypnotized. The study at http://med.stanford.edu/ism/2012/october/hypnotize.html means that 75% of the people you will deal with will be at susceptible to erotic hypnosis and the Hypno Poems. Pretty good odds I would say.

7 Kinds of Women Least Susceptible to Hypnotic Seduction

The are some personality types to be aware of when contemplating using Hypno Poems. You are unlikely to be successful with Women who exhibit these characteristics :
- o cynical or sarcastic (doesn't believe good things are possible)
- o low self-esteem (doesn't deserve good things to happen to her)
- o ADD (can't get or keep her attention)
- o won't shut up (can't get or keep her attention)
- o negative responder (counters everything you say with a negative response)
- o drunk or wasted (too unpredictable)
- o seriously depressed (you can't fix someone who needs psychotherapy with poems)

These Women Are the Best Bets for Hypnotic Seduction and Hypno Poems:

On the other hand, women who display these personality characteristics will be very susceptible to hypnosis and Hypno Poems:
- o good imagination and/or creative
- o responds well to whispered sexy talk
- o goes to "chick flicks" and romantic movies a lot with her girlfriends
- o reads romance novels – books by Harlequin in her bookcase
- o fond of "torch songs"
- o takes her a little time to get into the mood but does get into it eventually
- o tells you that you need to be more romantic, wants you to talk to her about "feelings"

Should I let her know that these are hypnotic poems?

I usually don't. Although if a woman is not fearful of being hypnotized, it will make them even more effective!

The word "hypnosis" seems to bring a lot of the negative associations about manipulation and doing things against one's will that it is best to do without – especially in the early stages of a relationship. You will end up talking about "hypnosis" and never doing it, and perhaps creating some resistance that you don't need. And, some puritanical types might think using hypnosis for seduction is somehow "creepy".

Now, if you have a trusting, long term relationship where you and your partner are into trying different things and open to experimentation, by all means, let them know. The hypnotic poems will definitely enhance her feelings for you, and some of them (like "Manzana", and "The Key") are specifically designed to amplify sexual desire and passion.

How do I bring these up in conversation?

Here are some ways you can bring these up:

- "A friend sent me these poems that he claims are kind of special. He said his girl really liked them and I was wondering how much you will enjoy hearing them…"
- "I don't know if you are the kind of person who really likes poetry, but I read a poem the other day and it made me think of you… would you like to hear it? (Be prepared to say why it made you think of them – "Oh, I don't know, something about reminded me of what a deep person you are – not like some of those other superficial women."
- "Do you know anyone who writes poetry (chances are she does)? I found these poems on the internet and I don't know what to make of them. I think you are pretty sharp, so maybe you can tell me how well you like them."
- "I don't normally like poetry or even get what most of it is all about. But, my friend Phil told me that most girls love it, especially the poetry that talks about real feelings and emotions. I don't know if I believe all that, but if I were to offer to read one of them to you, is that something you would be curious about?"

Can you use these in a bar or coffee shop?

Well, she has to be able to hear you and be in a situation where she is willing to pay attention to you. If not, do something else and try again later.

However, coffee shops are great place to introduce them, especially if it is attached attached to a bookstore like Barnes and Noble or Borders. Chances are any woman you find there will likely be a good possibility.

Bars are not so good, unless it is a quiet little place where you could carry on an intimate conversation. I was in a hotel bar one night listening to some jazz. There was one woman at the bar and probably 10 other guys, but no one had approached her. I went over and said:

" Hi, I don't mean to interrupt you, but I need your help with something. There is a woman I like at work and I wrote/found this poem that I was thinking about sharing with her. Would you listen to it and tell me what you think?"

We spent the next hour or so talking before calling it an evening. I did not try to close her for various reasons, but she definitely got into the poetry and it was having an effect. The other guys were checking us out and I am sure wondering what "line" I had used!

Do Hypno Poems Work on Men?

Using Hypnopoetics Erotic Hypnosis and Hypnotic Seduction Poetry on Men

I have received quite a few emails asking if these covert hypnosis patterns work only on women or do hypnosis poems work on men as well as women. Speed Seduction™ works on women because that is how Ross Jeffries designed it. Hypno Poems are hypnotic poetry that works extremely well on women, because that is how I designed them. Having said that, the Hypno Poems also work on men.

In this **Seducer's Guide**, and in the Hypno Poems, I use the feminine gender to refer to the person who is listening to the poem. If your spouse/lover/heart's desire is not female, feel free to read the poems with whatever gender is more appropriate to your situation.

Here is a series of emails that I received, with my responses - and the results the woman reported:

Hi,

I bought your ebook of hypnopoetics, and i notice it only describes how to read poetry to get a women to fall in love with you, My question is will it help me? (a women desperate to get her live in boyfriend to fall madly in love as he was in the beginning).

Do i read a poem a day, of course the ones that apply to me such as:
Coming to love
Will I know you
Healing
Truly See
Another time.

So I read one ever day?, or can i read all of them in one night? and how long do i keep reading the poems?

Thanks
Anon

Hi Anon –

Thanks for the purchase. These erotic hypnosis and hypnotic seduction poems were originally written to create the feelings in women, but I have found an interesting thing happening.

I recently recommended a sequence of Hypno Poems to a guy who was trying to win back his wife - they were on the brink of divorce. He had bought my book and after using the poems I suggested, things have gotten much better for them. So here is what he said:

"That day on the airport she stared at me for long periods with a smile on her face. We kissed in front of all the people and she just looked so happy after that...I went through the gates and I board the plane after that. Me myself feel also much relaxed...that poetry had a influence on myself...because now I see her through new eyes!!"

The key here is the changes he felt after using the poetry. So here is my idea: Have your guy read them to you. Just tell him you found this poetry that really seems different and special to you and that you would like to hear them read aloud by a guy. (If he isn't enough of a sport to read to you, blow him off and find someone with some soul!). Have him read two or three to you one evening (slowly and with feeling!) maybe while he is holding you in his arms. Ask him if he has ever felt that way, ask him to remember how things were when you were first together and how exciting it was as you were falling for each other. Then maybe reread them or some new ones to you on the next night.

You should be prepared to experience some really strong feelings as he reads them, but you will see that they affect him as well, as he goes through the process of romancing you with the poetry. I imagine you will both get fairly steamy pretty quick. Use them as often as you like, couldn't hurt. And, in general, guys respond well to direct physical affection, very visually oriented (what you wear and how you look), and really like to feel that they are appreciated. Write back and let me know how well this works for you and if you need more ideas...

Thanks again!
Phil

Hi Phil

Anon again, how long will i start seeing results? do i have him read the poems every time? or can i take turns?

Thanks
Anon

Anon –

Pay attention to the look on his face as he reads them, and as you read them to him. When he is looking a little dreamy-eyed or "spaced-out" you know they are working on him – these indicate a how deeply he is going into trance. Keep an eye out for changes in attitude or behavior over the next couple of weeks that will indicate that his feelings for you are growing stronger and deeper.

Taking turns should get the best results. Usually I can tell a difference in how someone feels about me after reading the erotic hypnosis and hypnotic seduction poems to them 3 or 4 times. Different people will have different responses, as you might expect, but anyone who is at all suggestible should start feeling pretty affectionate toward you after a half-dozen or so readings.

The Hypno Poem that is least about giving Embedded Commands and most about getting someone into trance is "Ocean Sunset". If that one doesn't trance him out, I will totally be surprised.

thanks,
Phil

Phil

"After reading to him for 3 nights in a row, amazingly his behavior was "WOW" ... what a change!! this man has stopped giving me affection for almost a year, and suddenly he starts being the affectionate man i met. So, I stopped reading, and sure enough the attention stopped. Am i going crazy?"

Anon

I cannot tell you how flattered I am when I receive Hypno Poems that my readers have written, or receive questions about how to write them.

So, here is a brief intro to how to write your own:
1. Determine what Stage the relationship is in – click here
2. Decide what emotional or belief state your partner is in and what state/belief you want to move them to
3. Write several lines that are meant to induce a dreamlike, trancelike or hypnotic state
4. Use, Covert Hypnosis, Conversational Hypnosis, Underground Hypnosis and NLP Language Patterns to start changing beliefs, imbedding commands, creating presuppositions, etc.... to create the body of the poem. (see Influence Phrases below).
5. It isn't so important to 'bring them out' of the trance. Having them kind of spacy and suggestible is good for further conversation hypnosis purposes
6. Always nice to bring the poem to a close with some little twist or hook.

The following is a list of NLP based "Influence phrases" and a list of Embedded Command "setup" phrases to use when writing your own Hypno Poems. You will find instances of most of these in my Hypno Poems. There are many more that you can find with a little research, but these will get you started:

Use These Influence Phrases

Just fill in the blanks with the action or benefit that you want your listener to take. In =some cases, you need to add a condition for the person to take the action. For instance, if you want them to fall in love with you try something like "You're interested in _falling in love_, aren't you" or "You can _fall in love_ because _it is the most natural thing to do_".

- You're interested in _____, aren't you?
- It's easy to _____ when _____, isn't it?
- The fact that _____, that _____, and that _____ means that _____.
- I know that _____ is important. I also know that _____ is important, too..
- It's not important that you _____, what's important is _____.
- When I _____, I said to myself, "_____."
- My friend Julia told me, "My mother always said, '_____.'"
- I would like to suggest that you take a moment to remember _____.
- If I _____ then we can _____. Does that seem fair enough?
- It's important to _____ is it not?
- You're going to feel delighted when you find out _____.

7

- I'm not going to tell you that _____, because that's something that you want to find out for yourself.
- I'm not going to say: "_____", because that would just be arrogant.
- You can _____ because _____.
- Some people say to me "_____", but I know that _____.
- I understand how you feel. My friend Jackie felt the same way, but she found that _____.
- Sometimes, when _____, I ask "_____?" but with other people I wait and see.
- When people like yourself finds _____, they are able to _____.

Set Up Embedded Commands Like This

You can use these phrases to set up embedded commands in your own Hypno Poems. Using the "fall in love" example above, you might use "What's it like when you *fall in love*?".

- Luckily you can _____
- You might want to _____
- I wouldn't tell you _____
- When you _____
- If you were to _____
- If I were to _____
- What's it like when you _____
- A person can _____
- It's not necessary to _____
- You really shouldn't _____
- You don't have to _____
- You can _____

By adding the word "Now" at the end of the Embedded command amplifies the effect. For instance: "You really shouldn't: give in so easily – now".

Another way to amplify the effect is to say the command in a "command voice". There is a difference in your intonation between when you ask a question and give a command. Try asking aloud "Fall in love??" as a question, then try it again as a command: "Fall in love!!". When you are reading a Hypno Poem, the person will be more likely to be influenced if you use the 2nd intonation. Their conscious mind will never notice, but their unconscious mind will pick up on it.

Here is that video on Embedded Commands again:
https://www.youtube.com/watch?v=8FlqNwEJZLk

Presuppositions – a presupposition   is when a statement or ask a question requires her unconscious mind to accept the truth of something in order to make sense of the question or statement. It is easier to show than to explain.

Examples of presuppositions include:

- You want a lover who listens to you
  - o Presupposition – you want a lover
- You are ready to start having some real fun"
  - o Presupposition – you have NOT been having real fun .
- Have you stopped enjoying that kind of pleasure?
  - o Presupposition – you once enjoyed that kind of pleasure
- When your boyfriend disses you it hurts
  - o Presupposition: you have a boyfriend who disses you and hurts you

Since Hypno Poems are designed to move someone from one emotional/belief state to another, you will not be surprised to find that some hypno poems are especially useful at different Stages of a relationship.

The following list of poems has four topics listed for each poem, to give you some insight as to:
- which stage of a relationship a particular Hypno Poem is particularly effective,
- the message, purpose, intent or Speed Seduction pattern of the poem
- the Doorways into the Unconscious that the poem utilizes
- the Embedded Commands (post-hypnotic suggestions) used in the poem

Relationship Stage

The first topic identifies which Stage of a relationship that the specific Hypno Poem is most effective. If you are already in a sexual relationship , most any poem is a good poem to use. The relationship Stages are as follows:
- **Any Stage**
- **Just Met and Early Stage these poems create intrigue, interest, comfort, safety, and sense of connection)**
- **Love/Sexual/Seduction (these move her from connection and comfort to sexual interest and desire, command her to fall in love with you, and create a strong sexual desire for you, and these are strong sexual accelerators that ramp up desire in an existing relationship or marriage)**
- **End of Relationship (these provide closure to a relationship that is ending)**

Message, Purpose, Intent, Pattern

This is pretty self-explanatory, except that "**Pattern**" is the Ross Jeffries Speed Seduction Pattern modeled by the Hypno Poem, where applicable.

Doorways into the Unconscious Mind

The third topic listed details which of the "**Doorways to the Unconscious Mind**" are being employed in the poem. Ross Jeffries, in his Speed Seduction Home Study Course, says there are four doorways into a woman's unconscious mind:
- **Internal Body sensations** – get her focused on internal sensations such as a feeling of warmth flowing through her chest, the feeling of her heart pounding with excitement, etc.
- **Emotional connections -** get her feeling emotionally connected, feeling strong, deep, positive emotions, connected to you
- **Getting her to start visualizing -** get her to visualize scenes of romance, terrific sex or fantasies
- **Elicit her deeper belief structures and values -** require her to access the core level of her identity so you can associate the positive values and beliefs with you

Of course, the more of these you can access, the better.

Embedded Commands

Embedded Commands are authoritative commands or suggestions that are given to someone who is preferably in a hypnotic trance state. In most cases, the Embedded commands in Hypno Poems are intended to get an immediate response. Sometimes, the Embedded Commands are post-hypnotic and are intended to trigger responses that will affect her behavior for days to a lifetime in duration.

Here is a short video that covers the concept fairly well. It is oriented to "sales", which is really the same as "persuasion", which is what these poems do for you: http://www.youtube.com/watch?v=8FlqNwEJZLk. Note – I have not purchased and am not endorsing this guy's products, I just think he does a good job in the video.

I suggest that when you are reading the poems to someone, you use a lower, sexier voice when saying the command, and if possible, connect with eye contact at the same time. Guaranteed to produce Global Warming of her lady parts.

Please refer to Appendix A for a complete list of the Embedded Commands in the Poems.

It's a Pretty Easy Decision

So, if you want to use a poem that would be good early in a relationship, and that works very much like Ross Jeffries' **"Instantaneous Connection Pattern"**, and gives her post-hypotic suggestions like "Feel the attraction growing", then you would pick **"In an Instant"**.

Relationship Stage: Any Stage
Message, Purpose, Intent, Pattern: Take her into trance, create sense of intrigue, feelings of comfort and safety, drop inhibitions and anchor all these good feelings to you.
Doorways to the Unconscious:
- o Guided Visualization
- o Generate Internal Body Sensations

Embedded Commands:
- o you can imagine
- o (I will) enter and warm you
- o open your heart to me
- o you will want to know me
- o you will want to hold me
- o you will give me that lover's special gift
- o let yourself fall
- o try (and fail) to resist
- o allow yourself to experience this moment
- o feel your inhibitions melt
- o notice your feelings changing for me

Relationship Stage: Just Met, Any Stage
Message, Purpose, Intent, Pattern: Get into her dream place, have her fantasize sex acts and associate them to you
Doorways to the Unconscious:
- o Elicit her deeper belief structures and values
- o Guided Visualization
- o Generate Internal Body Sensations
- o Build and Strengthen Emotional Connections

Embedded Commands:
- o remember a time
- o think of a love
- o find me there

Relationship Stage: Any Stage
Message, Purpose, Intent, Pattern: Guided Visualization to create romantic mood, build and strengthen connection, have her follow your lead

Doorways to the Unconscious:
- o Guided Visualization
- o Generate Internal Body Sensations
- o Build and Strengthen Emotional Connections

Embedded Commands:
- o sets your mind adrift
- o you want (it) to last
- o linger a moment
- o (you are) swept away
- o let yourself fall
- o allow yourself to believe
- o open your heart
- o can you come
- o you suddenly know

Moment of Grace

Relationship Stage: Just Met, Any Stage

Message, Purpose, Intent, Pattern: Guided Visualization to create romantic mood, build and strengthen connection, have her follow your lead.

Doorways to the Unconscious:
- o Elicit her deeper belief structures and values
- o Guided Visualization
- o Generate Internal Body Sensations
- o Build and Strengthen Emotional Connections

Embedded Commands:
- o your heart is swelled
- o (you are) filled with those feelings
- o (you) feel the music
- o focus on things unseen
- o (you) feel a yearning that you must satisfy

Right now

Relationship Stage: Any Stage

Message, Purpose, Intent, Pattern: Quick Induction to get her to open her heart to you, right now and to believe that this was meant to be

Doorways to the Unconscious:
- o Generate Internal Body Sensations
- o Build and Strengthen Emotional Connections

Embedded Commands:

14

- o feel yourself being drawn…willingly
- o let yourself go
- o surrender to those feelings
- o choose to do this
- o give yourself over
- o come to understand

Relationship Stage: Just Met, Early Stages
Message, Purpose, Intent, Pattern: Create intrigue and a strong, instantaneous emotional connection - similar to the Instantaneous Connection Pattern by Ross Jeffries. Uses an "Elman Induction" to induce trance.
Doorways to the Unconscious:
- o Elicit her deeper belief structures and values
- o Guided Visualization
- o Generate Internal Body Sensations
- o Build and Strengthen Emotional Connections

Embedded Commands:
- o feel it… see it… hear it
- o you have no choice
- o feel the attraction growing
- o see illumination
- o hear communication
- o sit and talk
- o discover the miracle
- o just stop
- o imagine a time
- o know you will be together
- o know that you have found
- o acknowledge you are ready
- o accept the time has come
- o say yes… say yes… say yes

Relationship Stage: Love/Sexual/Seduction
Message, Purpose, Intent, Pattern: Clarity trances her out and gets her to imagine a romantic interlude. It is especially effective for visually oriented women, and is useful in getting her to forget about any past hurts or disappointments so she can have a relationship with you.
Doorways to the Unconscious:

- o   Elicit her deeper belief structures and values
- o   Guided Visualization
- o   Generate Internal Body Sensations
- o   Build and Strengthen Emotional Connections

Embedded Commands:
- o   picture this
- o   watch that image grow
- o   find yourself dreaming
- o   imagine yourself spending
- o   picture… intimate scenes
- o   see your life is ready… a different perspective
- o   watch the past… fade

Unvalentine

Relationship Stage: Early Stages

Message, Purpose, Intent, Pattern: Not really a hypnotic poem, but is useful in setting the expectations for the relationship.

Doorways to the Unconscious:
- o   N/A

Embedded Commands:
- o   N/A

Manzana

Relationship Stage: Love/Sexual/Seduction

Message, Purpose, Intent, Pattern: This is a sexual accelerator which stimulates her sexually and has her imagine having and enjoying oral sex with you. It is similar to the "Blow Job" Pattern of Ross Jeffries.

Doorways to the Unconscious:
- o   Guided Visualization
- o   Generate Internal Body Sensations

Embedded Commands:
- o   you want (this)
- o   imagine dropping clothing
- o   imagine … heat
- o   imagine… relaxing
- o   you are sinking… surrendering
- o   decide the time has come
- o   close your eyes
- o   pause and tease
- o   anticipate… kiss

- o feel attraction's pull
- o (you will) discover and enjoy

The Difference

Relationship Stage: Early Stages

Message, Purpose, Intent, Pattern: This poem is designed to make her decide to have a relationship with you by challenging her model of what is possible. It is especially useful when she is definitely interested in getting it on with you, but is hesitating or indecisive about doing so.

Doorways to the Unconscious:
- o Elicit her deeper belief structures and values

Embedded Commands:
- o decide to believe
- o do this (even though)
- o choose to do it

Coming to Love

Relationship Stage: Love/Sexual/Seduction

Message, Purpose, Intent, Pattern: This poem is to move her from the initial stages of attraction to falling in love with you. It works best when she already knows, trusts, and is comfortable with you. It is a good "friends to lovers" poem.

Doorways to the Unconscious:
- o Guided Visualization
- o Build and Strengthen Emotional Connections

Embedded Commands:
- o feel... attraction
- o know the process has begun
- o realize you can
- o feel yourself fall
- o just give in
- o give yourself
- o feel the magical and miraculous

Certainly

Relationship Stage: Love/Sexual/Seduction

Message, Purpose, Intent, Pattern: Induction to create instant connection, generate sexy feelings and secure her permission to proceed

Doorways to the Unconscious:
- o Generate Internal Body Sensations
- o Build and Strengthen Emotional Connections

Embedded Commands:
- o feel the glow
- o enjoy the warmth
- o say "yes"

How Will I Know You?

Relationship Stage: Just Met, Early Stages

Message, Purpose, Intent, Pattern: She has found what she is looking for – you. Also has some future pacing.

Doorways to the Unconscious:
- o Generate Internal Body Sensations
- o Build and Strengthen Emotional Connections

Embedded Commands:
- o show me
- o you are… attracted to me
- o feel… connection
- o know… it is real
- o try (and fail) to resist
- o (you) fall into… love
- o remember this
- o fall…willingly

Reciprocity

Relationship Stage: Any Stage

Message, Purpose, Intent, Pattern: Mirroring her for rapport building. Especially effective with kinesthetic oriented women.

Doorways to the Unconscious:
- o Guided Visualization
- o Generate Internal Body Sensations
- o Build and Strengthen Emotional Connections

Embedded Commands:
- o feel delight
- o your heart is ready to open
- o energy flows into you

Touch

Relationship Stage: Love/Sexual/Seduction

Message, Purpose, Intent, Pattern: This is a sexual accelerator which stimulates her sexually. It works best when she already knows, trusts, and is comfortable with you. It is a good "friends to lovers" poem. Especially effective for kinesthetic oriented women.

Doorways to the Unconscious:
- o Guided Visualization
- o Generate Internal Body Sensations

Embedded Commands:
- o feel yourself longing for touch
- o imagine lips pressing
- o fit so well
- o awaken feelings
- o remember that sudden rush
- o feel so alive
- o your breathing … deeper and faster
- o there is room … in your heart … opening in your life

To Truly See

Relationship Stage: Just Met, Early Stages

Message, Purpose, Intent, Pattern: Changes her mind if she thinks that you are not her type

Doorways to the Unconscious:
- o Elicit her deeper belief structures and values
- o Build and Strengthen Emotional Connections

Embedded Commands:
- o find yourself looking beyond
- o see something
- o something … touches you deep inside
- o know you are connecting
- o feel connected in this way – now
- o stop and feel safe … excited
- o feel secure … longing, passion and desire
- o imagine … happiness and pleasure

Lion and the Rose

Relationship Stage: Love/Sexual/Seduction

Message, Purpose, Intent, Pattern: Guided Visualization to create romantic mood and acts as a sexual accelerator and stimulant.

Doorways to the Unconscious:
- o Guided Visualization

o   Generate Internal Body Sensations
Embedded Commands:
  o   n/a

Relationship Stage: Love/Sexual/Seduction
Message, Purpose, Intent, Pattern: Guided Visualization to create romantic mood and acts as a sexual accelerator and stimulant.
Doorways to the Unconscious:
  o   Elicit her deeper belief structures and values
  o   Guided Visualization
  o   Generate Internal Body Sensations
Embedded Commands:
  o   feel the strength and energy
  o   find the bliss
  o   imagine someone

Relationship Stage: Any Stage
Message, Purpose, Intent, Pattern: To get her to release any negative emotions and associations that she may have regarding something that happened in her past. This could be past hurt or something involving you or someone else, Lets her put the past behind her and feel ready for a new, passionate relationship with you.
Doorways to the Unconscious:
  o   Elicit her deeper belief structures and values
  o   Guided Visualization
  o   Generate Internal Body Sensations
  o   Build and Strengthen Emotional Connections
Embedded Commands:
  o   your heart is ready to trust
  o   your soul is ready to heal
  o   your body is ready to feel ... hope and passion
  o   place your hand on the knob
  o   you are ready now to fill that space within
  o   loneliness is finished
  o   your happiness can begin;
  o   know that now you have ... found
  o   feel beginning to grow
  o   you have already made that choice
  o   hear something special

- o listen to a voice
- o remove all your fear
- o you have chosen to live
- o you have chosen to give

Another Time

Relationship Stage: Love/Sexual/Seduction
Message, Purpose, Intent, Pattern: Not her type pattern, challenge her to not care what others think
Doorways to the Unconscious:
- o Elicit her deeper belief structures and values
- o Guided Visualization
- o Generate Internal Body Sensations
- o Build and Strengthen Emotional Connections

Embedded Commands:
- o you know ... love is there
- o your heart knows
- o the connection you feel
- o you know this ... is perfect
- o feel connected ... understood
- o you know it will be good

Locket

Relationship Stage: End
Message, Purpose, Intent, Pattern: This poem is intended to end a relationship in a positive way. It leaves open the possibility of resuming the relationship in the future – with all the positive aspects preserved. It might also be useful as a way to bring up the possibility that the relationship might end,
Doorways to the Unconscious:
- o Elicit her deeper belief structures and values
- o Guided Visualization
- o Generate Internal Body Sensations
- o Build and Strengthen Emotional Connections

Embedded Commands:
- o imagine a locket
- o imagine it down deep

21

eBook Review of "Hypnopoetics…Modern Love Poems and Hypnotic Inductions" by Phil Billitz

Reviewed by: Matthew McKenzie, Certified Hypnotherapist

Ever wished for a book of covert hypnotic seduction patterns so well hidden they seemed natural, effortless and completely above board? Asking for a bit much you might say, or a little too hard to get all in one place you might think. Well I've been searching for that very thing myself, as a certified hypnotherapist and a poet, I've searched and searched for materials that would create a harmonic blend of hypnotic poetry and deliver emotionally charged hypnotic poems.

You couldn't believe how much PUA junk and erotic hypnosis mumbo jumbo I had to run through to even get some decent information. Even then I was still struggling to come up with anything even remotely effective, and without any decent examples this dream was stalling in its tracks…

So when I ran across Phil's site, I was floored, here was the answer! After doing some research I found the entire internet had nothing even remotely negative to say about him, and aside from some pheromone ads (which I personally find the concept a bit shady) I was intrigued and determined to be open minded about what he had to offer. So after signing up for his newsletter on the selling page I emailed him.

With a quick response I found Phil charming and honest. He sent me the product for review and I eagerly downloaded the book. I was stunned at the beauty of his product, both aesthetically and as a fellow lover of words and linguistic patterns. He has created a wonderful collection of hypnotic poems both in a form to be read electronically with an introduction to his work and it's nature, and also (here's the kicker) the same just as hypnotic poems in a print ready form so you can have a harmless looking book of poems to read from to the lucky receiver of your choice!

That's the great thing about these poems, they're written to someone special. From the stable role of a secure and enticing leader, not from the sappy whining place of a desperate lovesick guy needing validation. You also get the benefit of the doubt, if things don't go over well; it's not your poem, not your problem. It's really a win-win scenario!

The other bonus, *Seducer's Guide to Hypnopoetics* was the only minor let down, and this was only because I myself was looking for something other than what Phil had presented. It's a work in progress for goodness sakes, where are my manners?

Anyway, personally I am interested in being able to create such works on my own, and while the other two books offer great templates to study and analyze I wanted some instruction on how to create hypnotic poetry myself.

While this added bonus is a great guide to select which poem from the book to read for what purpose, or stage of the relationship as well as illustrating the embedded commands in the poems, it holds no instructional material. That's not to say he's got a great product to offer, I just had some unreasonably high expectations about that part of the deal.

He also includes as an added bonus, an audio book version of the poems showing you how to read them for maximum hypnotically seductive impact. Imagine being able to put your special someone into a deliciously relaxed and erotically charged state just by having him or her listen to these recordings!

In summary, Phil has put together a terrific collection of poems for you and it'd be a shame to miss out on this wonderful opportunity.

Matthew McKenzie, Certified Hypnotherapist

Note from Phil – This Second Edition of the "Seducer's Guide" addresses the shortcomings that Matthew raises in his review.

What Women are Saying About Hypnopoetics

Click here to read What Women are Saying About "Hypnopoetics…"

What Men are Saying About Hypnopoetics

Click here to read What Men are Saying About "Hypnopoetics…"

Watch These Videos

I have created some videos on YouTube to show you how you might introduce the idea od reading the poems to someone. They are fairly amateurish, and I apologize for that. I am definitely a much better poet and hypnotist than I am a videographer.

- Hypnosis - How to Hypnotize Women - Seducer's Guide Pt.1
- Hypnosis - How to Hypnotize Women You Have Just Met - Seducer's Guide Pt.2
- Hypnosis - How to Hypnotize Your Wife or GF - Seducer's Guide Pt.3

Other Resources

- Wiki article on Hypnosis Susceptibility
- Ross Jeffries Speed Seduction Products
- Hypnotic Suggestion

Thank You!

Thank you for buying and reading this book and trusting me to offer something of value. I sincerely hope you use these concepts to get more of what you really want from a partner – whatever that means to you.

By now you understand what is happening in these Hypno Poems and appreciate why this poetry is so powerful. Because there are dozens of poems to use at all **stages of a relationship**, you will want to get the entire collection.

If all this talk of Embedded commands, presuppositions and Neurol inguistics seems a bit intellectual and geeky to you, all you need to know is that, as many people are finding out, "It **really works!!**"

And I hope you start writing your own Hypno Poems and that you are even more wildly successful than I have been using these techniques.

I know I have often complained about being waaaay too busy.

This is one thing to know for sure – I am always thrilled to hear from you about your experiences using Hypno Poems and "Hypnopoetics…"

You know the drill! Go to my website, http://www.hypnopoetics.com , and sign up for my FREE "Unfair Advantage" newsletter.

That's how our friendship will start, if we are not already great friends.

I hope you'll consider subscribing to my blog at http://speed-seduction-bonus.com/nlpseduction/ You can sign up for The "Unfair Advantage" Newsletter there as well.

And for facebook fans, stop by http://www.facebook.com/hypnotic.seduction. Click "Like" and you can get more Hypno Poems – both pdf and mp3 versions.

It would be a huge honor if you decide to subscribe or "Like" my pages. That would prove that this book had a positive impact on YOU.

Naturally, I would also love for you to buy one of my books and use it to romance your partner when you need a little help in setting the mood or closing the deal.

And, even if you choose not to, we can still be friends, yes?
best always,
Phil

- **Never use Hypnotic Poetry to Manipulate People!**
- **Always use Hypnopoetics ethically!**
- **Never read Hypnotic Poetry to someone who is driving!**

Postscript 10/09/2008 – New for ver 2.0 - Cover Page, explanation of charts. This is all for version 2.0. Future revisions will at have the Embedded commands for the last 6 poems. I will add another section that will illustrate some seduction strategies that can be implemented as a sequence of poems. When read in sequence they will capture and lead the woman's imagination exactly where you want it to go.

Postscript 5/19/2014 – New for ver3.2 – completely filled out the Embedded commands and listed the poems in the order that they appear in "Hypnopoetics…Modern Love Poems and Hypnotic Inductions"

- provided FAQ
- provided links to videos with examples of how to use the poems

Poem Title	Embedded Commands Used In The Poem
Ocean Sunset	you can imagine enter and warm you you open your heart to me you will want to know me you will want to hold me you will give me that lover's special gift let yourself fall try (and fail) to resist allow yourself to experience this moment feel your inhibitions melt notice your feelings changing for me
Sublimity	remember a time think of a love find me there i have entered
Milonguero	sets your mind adrift you want to last linger a moment swept away let yourself fall allow yourself to believe open your heart can you come you suddenly know flowing into you
Moment of Grace	your heart is swelled (you are) filled with those feelings you feel the music focus on things unseen (you) feel a yearning that you must satisfy
Right now	this was meant to be feel yourself being drawn…willingly let yourself go surrender to those feelings choose to do this give yourself over come to understand open your heart… right now

In an Instant	feel it... see it... hear it
	you have no choice
	feel the attraction growing
	see illumination
	hear communication
	sit and talk
	discover the miracle
	you can just stop
	imagine a time
	know you will be together
	know that you have found
	acknowledge you are ready
	accept the time has come
	say yes... say yes... say yes
Clarity	picture this
	watch that image grow
	find yourself dreaming
	imagine yourself spending
	picture... intimate scenes
	see your life is ready... a different perspective
	watch the past... fade
Unvalentine	share long slow holding
	let me ... be your lover
Manzana	you want... this
	imagine dropping...clothing
	imagine the heat
	imagine... relaxing
	you are sinking... surrendering
	decide the time has come
	close your eyes
	pause and tease
	anticipate... kiss
	feel attraction's pull
	you will discover and enjoy
The Difference	decide to believe
	do this even though
	choose to do it
	you have chosen
Coming to Love	feel... attraction
	know the process has begun
	realize you can
	feel yourself fall
	just give in
	give yourself
	feel the magical and miraculous
Certainly	feel the glow
	enjoy the warmth
	the longing builds
	say "yes"

How Will I Know You?	show me
	you are... attracted to me
	feel... connection
	know that it is real
	try to resist
	you fall into... love
	you will remember this
Reciprocity	warms your heart
	feel delight
	your heart is ready to open
	energy flows into you
Touch	feel yourself longing for touch
	imagine lips pressing
	they fit so well
	they awaken feelings
	remember that sudden rush
	feel so alive
	your breathing ... deeper and faster
	there is room ... in your heart ... opening in your life
To Truly See	you find yourself looking beyond
	you can see something
	you know you are connecting
	feel connected in this way – now
	stop and feel safe ... excited
	feel secure ... longing, passion and desire
	imagine ... happiness and pleasure
Lion and The Rose	n/a
Pegasus	feel the strength and energy
	find the bliss
	imagine someone
Healing	your heart is ready to trust
	your soul is ready to heal
	your body is ready to feel ... hope and passion
	imagine yourself placing your hand on the knob
	you are ready now to fill that space within
	know that now you have ... found
	you have already made that choice
	hear something special
	listen to a voice
	remove all your fear
	you have chosen to live
	you have chosen to give
Another Time	you know ... love is there
	your heart knows
	the connection you feel... is real
	you know this ... is perfect
	feel connected ... understood
	you know it will be good
Locket	imagine a locket
	imagine it down deep

The following is the Original Foreword to "Hypnopoetics...Modern Love Poems and Hypnotic Inductions":

"Hypnotic poems are certainly not new. Since the beginning of time, some poetry has had a profoundly hypnotic effect. Its rhythm, meter, rhyme and cadence are such that its recitation has a mesmerizing effect. And certainly my favorite poems have always been those that capture and lead the imagination.

But what would happen if one were to intentionally combine the language and technology of hypnosis and the language of poetry to produce a specific state of mind in the listener? Well, you would end up with this book.

I was trying to explain the poems in this book to a literary agent one day, and after describing them as best I could, I finally said: "Look, there is something you need to know about these poems. They are not really poems at all. They are hypnotic inductions that use the language of hypnosis and Neuro-Linguistic Programming to program a woman's unconscious mind to make her fall hopelessly in love with you."

After looking at me, looking at the manuscript and looking back at me, all he could think of to say was, "Should I be creeped out by this?"

After I assured him that he would not be hypnotized and seduced if I were to read him some of them, I did so. His reaction was that he felt soothed and relaxed and not at all in love with me, but was intrigued and wanted to find out more.

So you, dear reader, may end up wondering the same thing. To answer that right away, no, you shouldn't feel creeped out at all. But you may find yourself feeling intrigued, captivated and motivated to read and understand them. And perhaps becoming interested in learning more about the language patterns and technology used in them.

Which brings us to an important point about hypnotism: hypnosis can only persuade a person to do what they were always willing to do in the first place. If you don't want to dance like a chicken no hypnotic power on earth is going to get you scratching around in the dirt.

Hypnopoetics

Hypnopoetics works in a similar way. If a woman is totally closed to romance, or is physically repelled by your lack of hygiene, you are probably not going to get her to quickly and hopelessly fall in love with you - no matter how good the poems are.

However, the good news is that in general, women love romance and want to fall in love. And they need to experience a sense of connection before they can find a man attractive and become emotionally and physically involved with him.

This poetry will create the connection and the attraction will follow. And it creates that connection, and more, by using the science and language of Hypnosis and NLP.

Poetry Based on the New Science of Instant Behavior Change

Neuro-linguistic Programming (NLP) was created by Dr. John Grinder and Richard Bandler on the campus of the University of California at Santa Cruz. Working together, the pair developed NLP - the most incredibly powerful change technology known to mankind.

Their books and techniques have helped thousands of people change their beliefs and their lives by overcoming Shyness, Procrastination, Fear and Doubt, Lack of Confidence, Test Anxiety, Fear of Public Speaking, and even get rid of the tragic effects of childhood trauma.

NLP produces powerful shifts in attitudes and behavior in a matter of minutes. People from all over the world studied their techniques because of their power to produce change. One of these students was Tony Robbins. Today, you see him on infomercials as the self-help guru of the world; but his roots are solidly based in NLP.

Bandler and Grinder invented techniques to model people who were experts in their field, and taught people how to achieve results just like the masters. And the techniques are often used in professional sports training programs. What would it be worth to have the golfing skills of Tiger Woods? What if you had the entrepreneurial drive of Bill Gates? What if you had the charisma of Mick Jagger?

One of the masters they modeled was Milton Ericson, probably the most famous and most effective hypnotist in the history of psychology. They studied and modeled his use of language to take people into and out of hypnotic trance, and to create immediate, dramatic changes in their beliefs and behavior just by talking to them.

The Use for NLP That They Don't Tell You About

There is another application for NLP that is equally as powerful as the ones above. But you won't read about it in m any books because it is considered too controversial. Even the people that use it often don't admit that is what they are doing. It is the use of NLP for romance and seduction.

Because, falling in love is a process, a process in which someone moves through a series of mental and emotional states. And like any internal process, NLP can be used to model and reproduce its results, and to capture and lead the imagination in such a way as to speed up the process so that it can happen in a matter of minutes instead of months.

This poetry is written using these NLP techniques. It is designed to change a woman's state of mind in the right order and sequence to lead her to where she has always wanted to go, to fall deeply and completely in love. To give credit where it is due, the first poetry of this kind that I became aware of was written by Ross Jeffries.

Now, I don't want to try to train you in NLP or Eriksonian hypnosis - the point is that these technologies work. And better yet they will work for you without knowing anything about either of these topics. That is the point of making these poems available to you - you don't have to know a thing about the technology. Simply start to use the poems and see the astounding results for yourself.

These poems can have a very powerful influence on the unconscious mind of the listener. How powerful is it? Think about falling deliriously in love in minutes instead of months. What if that could happen to you? Wouldn't you want to do that? Now?

Specifically, this beautiful poetry uses trance language, softeners, Embedded commands, tonality, universal experiences, Eriksonian hypnosis language patterns, covert communication techniques, and phonetic ambiguity. This powerful language is used in a way to evoke the process of falling in love, of increasing the passion and intensity of an existing relationship, to provide closure to the heart and soul after a relationship has ended.

These poems gently and gracefully change a woman's mental and emotional state to the state you desire without their awareness, and allow you to overcome resistance without argument, conflict or tension.

There is nothing unethical about using NLP to invite and lead someone into a closer relationship – people of both sexes are continually using cosmetics, clothing and fragrances to attract and keep love in their life. By using NLP, all you are doing, is simply creating the opportunity for them to experience that relationship in the most convincing, compelling, and psychologically-effective, way possible.

And, of course, that gives you an incredible advantage over your competitors in this game of Love…

Phil Billitz
2008

www.ingramcontent.com/pod-product-compliance
Lightning Source LLC
Chambersburg PA
CBHW070241290526
45789CB00004B/1710